NAVIGATING GRIEF WITH JESUS

By Sarah Wood-Bradford

PREFACE

I have been widowed twice, most recently on December 16, 2019. I am writing this in 2020, so it is still so fresh in my mind. I cannot imagine people losing loved ones, not knowing Jesus Christ as their Lord and Savior.

I use the word navigating because when you lose a spouse you can either stay on a course in life that is stable and sure like a ship that is shored up on a strong foundation, or you can flounder like a ship that has lost its way.

Writing this book will bring many tears recalling memories, but it will also I pray help others who read it to navigate their grief with hope.

People sometimes have a hard time looking at me and understanding why I am not falling apart, how I have joy at this moment in time.

The answer is Jesus Christ.

I

Everyone experiences grief at some point in their lives if they live long enough. Most of us will experience grief more than once, and I am only talking about grief associated with losing someone close to you. It can be a relative or a friend.

My first recollection of death was when I was about eight years old. My aunt died, my Mother took me to the funeral home to view her. I don't really remember experiencing much emotion other than I hated seeing other people cry. I did not know this aunt well since my family had very little contact with her. As a child of eight, I knew about God and heaven; didn't know about having a relationship with Jesus Christ. I probably just assumed she went to heaven because she was a "good" person. I didn't miss her since I really didn't have a relationship with her. I was just uncomfortable seeing a dead person in a casket and seeing people crying.

When I was twelve, the only Grandmother I ever knew died. My other grandparents had died before I was born. I had stayed with this Grandmother a lot, she even lived with my family for a while. I still didn't know about having a relationship with Jesus Christ. I was sad because I knew I would be missing her, but yet I don't really remember grieving. I think I was more uncomfortable with all the people coming to the house and seeing my Mother cry. It was her mother. Once again, I think I just assumed she went to heaven. I can look back and think about how children look at such events. As a child, I did not want people outside my family to see me cry; I was embarrassed by such emotion. I

was embarrassed by my mother's display of emotion; so I tended to hold mine in tightly.
Someone might want to analyze that; but I am not concerned with that, that is not what this book is about.

II

A real turning point in my life came when I was eighteen. I was a Freshman in college. I still did not have a relationship with Jesus Christ. The evening before my birthday I received a call in my dorm room from a friend of my mother's. He told me that my brother had been killed that afternoon in a gun accident. It felt as if someone had punched me in the gut and knocked all of the wind out of me. The friend was coming to pick me up at school, which was about a 3-hour drive. I remember lying on my bed, empty. I shut down. I don't remember outwardly having cried at this time, but I was crying inside.

My brother was fourteen at the time, in the eighth grade. He was my only living sibling. My mother had lost two children prior to me being born: one with bacterial meningitis, and one right after birth.

The ride home was long. I was so empty I could not carry on a conversation other than to ask what happened. My mother's friend told me that my brother and his friend had been in his friend's barn and somehow my brother's friend's shotgun accidently went off and hit my brother. He pretty much died right away. There were no other details.

My parents were in bed by the time I arrived home. I remember being scared because it made me realize that I was not guaranteed tomorrow; if my brother could die at fourteen, I could die at eighteen; and would I go to Heaven or Hell. I slept on the floor at the foot of my parents' bed that night and every night I was there. I guess I thought if I could somehow be close to them, I would be protected from death.

During that time was the only time I ever saw my father cry. My father was 84 at the time. He was a lot older than my mother and was having some health problems. He did not go to the funeral or the funeral home. I went with my mother to pick out the casket and make arrangements, and spend some time with my brother before the visitors came. It was hard standing in a receiving line making proper responses to people's condolences. The whole eighth class came also.

This all took place a few days before Thanksgiving so I was off some extra time before I had to go back to school. I had plenty of time to think about many things. I thought about my final resting place - heaven or hell. I thought about how little I knew about my brother. I have thought about it over the years and realize how self-centered I was at the time. I had not given my brother much thought when he was alive; I was more concerned about what was going on in my life. I didn't want to be bothered with him. I didn't even know he was on the basketball team until after he died - sad. I thought about the times I was hateful to him because I didn't want to talk to him.

I went to the school to pick up his belongings. The principal said it would be nice if I would talk to the boy who shot him and tell him we didn't blame him. I didn't say anything to my mother about that because at that time I think she might have blamed him. She could not fathom how it could have happened if the boy had not been careless. The details were sketchy, small town police ruled as a accident, and did not investigate further. If my mother found out more details, she never told me and I did not ask. The policeman did comment that where the bullet entered indicated my brother had his arm up. Maybe they were playing cops and robbers. It was a 410 shotgun, so apparently he bled out quickly. There were no cell phones or 911 back then.

III

I went back to school with a heavy heart. I knew I was missing something in my life and I knew it had to do with God. I was raised in church, both my parents were Christians. I had always had an affinity for the things of God. I think I realized in high school that I was missing something, I just couldn't put my finger on it. I was lonely. One can be lonely even when having a lot of people around them. I had an active life, but that lonely feeling I always had was that hole in my life that only Jesus can fill. I realized later that the Holy Spirit had been drawing me for some time, I just didn't put all the dots together and respond properly. After I graduated from high school, I moved out and lived on my own for a while until I went to college. Over the years going to church and revival meetings, I had seen many people be touched and walk the aisle to the altar. I looked at it as some supernatural, emotional experience. One day while I was living on my own I asked God, "when is this kind of experience ever going to happen to me".

A few months later, in the Spring, I was sitting in a study area of my dorm and saw a poster for Bible Study with information about knowing Jesus, that was being held weekly on campus. I decided to go. The groups sponsoring these studies were Campus Crusade for Christ and The Navigators. Someone there explained to me the Plan of Salvation, how to have Jesus Christ as my Lord and Savior. Everything became clear. No lightening bolt was going to strike me to let me know it was my time to walk the aisle. All I had to do was pray and ask Jesus to come into my life, repent of my sin, put my trust and faith in Him. **"For all have sinned and come short of the glory of God." Romans 3:23 "For God so** loved the **WORLD, THAT HE GAVE HIS ONLY BEGOTTEN Son, that whosoever believeth in him should not perish, but have everlasting life." John 3:16** I did not pray there that night; but when I got back to the dorm, I went to that secluded study spot again and prayed. I told Jesus I believed in Him, I asked Him to come into my life, I asked Him for forgiveness, and I surrendered my life to Him. The first thing I realized as soon as I did that was the undescribable peace that came over me.

My relationship with Jesus began in March 1971, when I was nineteen years old. I was no longer lonely.

IV

That summer I moved to Chicago and became involved in a church in the city. I publicly confessed Jesus Christ as my Lord and Savior, and was baptized. **"That if thou shalt confess with thy mouth the Lord Jesus, and shalt believe in thine heart that God hath raised him from the dead, thou shalt be saved." Romans 10:9**

I started teaching the primary Sunday School kids, ages first and second grades. I ended up staying in Chicago until the next summer, and went to a university there. I was on fire for the Lord. I wanted everyone to be as excited as me. This year was 1971, during the Jesus movement. I took my Bible to school with me along with salvation tracts. I became involved in a home Bible Study. I joined a young people's Christian group. We went door to door handing out tracts and talking to people about Jesus. There was no fear of rejection, we just wanted to share with others what Jesus was doing in our lives.

I ended up working in a Christian publishing house which surrounded me with Christian people and Christian materials. I went to a Billy Graham crusade in the Spring of 1972 and rededicated my life to the Lord.

In June of 1972, my father passed away, went to be with the Lord. My mother asked me to move back home. My mother had called me to the hospital near my home because my father was in ICU and was not doing well. I remember going into the ICU room to see him. He was awake, but weak; I told him he was going to be okay, I think more trying to convince myself. The doctors had put in a pacemaker and he had developed heart pneumonia. His heart was tired, it was ready to stop working. I think he knew his time was short and he was going to be with the Lord. Before I left the room I told him I loved him, something I don't remember ever doing before. He told me he loved me which I don't ever remember him doing before either, even though I had never doubted that he did. Our family was not real out in the open with feelings that way. A few hours later he went to be with the Lord. Once again I went with my mother to make funeral arrangements. It had been less than two years since my brother had passed. This time it was different, yes I was sad that my father was gone; but I did not have that feeling of helplessness that I had had when my brother was killed. The difference- I now had a relationship with the Lord. I knew my father was with the Lord. The Lord had given him 86 years, he was ready to go.

I went back to Chicago long enough to gather my belongings and move back home. I hated leaving my church family and my job in the Chicago area, but when I moved back home, I didn't hesitate to get involved in a new church. It is always important to stay plugged in with the Lord no matter where you are. **"Not forsaking the assembling of ourselves together..." Hebrews 10:25** Pray, and let the Lord show you where He wants you to worship. It was a trying year, living back home after having my independence; but God always makes a way.

V

1973 was a pivotal year. I got married and had my first child. My husband was someone who I had known for many years, and actually in my teenage-age years didn't like very much. It is funny how things can change, how the Lord can orchestrate things. I don't know whether or not Tom was who the Lord had intended me to marry. At the time I was 21 and had been a Christian not quite two years. I was not even aware that I should ask the Lord who He wanted me to marry. Tom and I had talked about the Lord while we were dating. I explained to him my relationship with Jesus. He told me he was baptized when he was ten. It was at a Baptist church. I just assumed at the time he knew Jesus. Whether or not he did at that time, I don't really know; I just know that it wasn't until many years later in our marriage that he really began to show fruit in his life. It was important to me at the time that he had a relationship with Jesus and I took his word for it. During the few short months we remained in Illinois after our marriage, I attended the church he grew up in. He did not attend now.

In 1974, we moved from our home state to the St. Louis area for Tom's job. As soon as we got to our new home, I found a church. Since becoming a Christian, that has always been very important to me, find a Body of Believers in which to worship. Tom attended sometimes. He was a professional musician at the time as well as holding another full-time job. We traveled a lot on weekends for his music as well as his playing at night during the week sometimes. My second child was born in 1974 also. We had a busy life.

In 1976, I decided to go back to school to finish my Bachelor of Science Degree. I went to night school so I could be at home during the day with my children, and Tom babysat them while I was at school. As well as school, I kept busy with church activities; attending home Bible Studies and helping with Vacation Bible School.

In 1977, my third child was born. God blessed me with my family. One thing I had always prayed for, even when I was a teenager, was to have children, to have a good family. I had always wanted five children, but realized after three that it would not be financially wise to do so. I wanted to be able to provide for our children comfortably and be able to provide them with different experiences when they were older. God showed me the wisdom of that.

I graduated with my Bachelor's Degree in 1978. I believe you would have called us an ordinary blue collar family at the time. Tom always worked, I was a stay-at-home mom. I believed and still do it is important for parents to raise their own children instead of day cares or babysitters. Yes, we struggled financially; but we always had food on the table, we owned a home, and we had the Lord in our lives. The sacrifice of not having things was worth it to be able to stay at home and raise my children myself. Did we do everything right, definitely not; but when we made a bad decision, we turned in a different direction, pulled our big boy and big girl pants up and moved forward. We did not wallow in self-pity or believe we were victims. We did not live on food stamps and government handouts. We did not have a new house, a new car, new furniture; but we had a whole lot of determination to live life as God intended.

VI

In 1978, after I received my degree, we bought a place with a little bit of acreage in the country west of St. Louis. My oldest child had just started Kindergarten. My husband commuted into the city for his job. By this time he had stopped playing music so much, he was tired of being on the road, and late nights. It was also trying to travel with three small children five and under.

I found a church I liked in the nearby community and continued my walk with the Lord. Tom found a job not far from our house so he did not have to commute into the city any longer. He also started a car detail business out of our garage and had the business of all the local car dealers. He found a church he liked and started going on a regular basis. He went a few times with the children and myself, but he liked the fire and brimstone preacher at this other church better. I did not mind, I was just glad he was worshiping the Lord.

The country life was good, family of five and a big overgrown St. Bernard. I got a horse, I had always loved horses from the time I was a little girl. I loved to ride, found a neighbor with which to ride. The kids had a pony.

When my middle child started first grade, I substitute taught some at her school. I also worked in the office some at a local hospital. My youngest enjoyed going to his babysitter, he had lots of kids with which to play. My hours were flexible so I was always home before my school kids got home.

It was at the church here, I started to pray out loud in a group. I had always before been scared to death of being called on to pray. I don't remember for sure, but I think it started with our Sunday School class having all members taking turns praying. I rehearsed in my mind what I was going to say, but it was a start. Praying between just myself and God was one thing, but in public was another. We all have to start somewhere.

Both my father-in-law and my mother passed away in 1980. My father-in-law had battled melanoma for about nine months. He was 57 when he died. He never came to the Lord until toward the end of his life while he was in the hospital. My mother died at the end of 1980 at age 60 from breast cancer. She had battled it for about 18 months. Ironically both my father-in-law and my mother found out about their cancers in the same month. She had known Jesus as her Lord and Savior for some years.

I believe the death of Tom's father hit him harder than he let on. My mother and I had had a somewhat of a rocky relationship. We were like oil and vinegar much of the time, but I felt she was at peace now. Her early years and the loss of three children always weighed heavily on her. God is merciful and spares us from a lot.

VII

In 1982, we decided to move back to our home state. After my mother's death, I inherited a house and a farm so we thought it best we move back into the area to be able to manage it better. We moved into one of the houses in which I grew up. My youngest was starting Kindergarten by this time. We stayed in this house for a year and moved to a town nearby where my husband had started a business. We would stay there nine years. I found a church there, Tom for the most part went back to not attending. He became engrossed in climbing the ladder. While in that church, my relationship with the Lord grew; I taught high school Bible Study, became the youth leader, and headed up the Christian Education Board. I started working a full-time job since all my children were in school. We led a busy lifestyle; myself between church activities and the children's school activities and social life, my husband between his business and our social activities.

In 1989, I decided to go back to school and get my Master's degree. I worked full time and went to school full time at night. I graduated in 1991, the same year my oldest graduated from high school, and my youngest from eighth grade.

We had gone on a trip a couple of times to New Orleans during these years and loved the area. We decided to move there in that summer of 1991. I had a job lined up that used my Master's education, and my husband had a job lined up. So, off we went. By this time Tom and I had been married eighteen years, and we had moved quite a few times. I guess we were kind of nomads at the time.

VIII

We moved to a suburb of New Orleans. My oldest was at a college in St. Louis, my middle child was starting her Junior year of high school, my youngest his first year of high school. It is still amazing to me how the Lord works, putting all the pieces together if you will just allow Him to be the pilot. My husband's boss lined us up with a real estate lady to find a rental house. This lady was also instrumental in guiding me to the church there in which I spent fifteen years. She was a member there.

My husband worked offshore so he was gone a lot. He did attend church with me some. He developed a good relationship with the pastor, and we socialized with he and his family outside of church. The fifteen years I spent at this church was such a great learning experience. I started teaching adult Bible Studies, had an adult Sunday School class, and did a lot of administrative work with the church. The second pastor I had while I was there was a great teacher as well as a pastor, I learned a lot from him. I had a great church family and many came to my house also for home Bible studies.

Once my husband turned 50, he started having some health problems. He quit smoking as he was having breathing problems, his breathing improved almost one hundred fold. But then he showed up diabetic. Having to squelch the urge to smoke and change his diet became a bondage for him. He did not go back to smoking, and he had given up alcoholic drinks some years before, but he ended up dealing with an eating disorder. He had not taken care of his body in earlier years, it was finally catching up with him.

About two years before he passed, he started going to a nondenominational church. He had allowed the ignorance of a few church members turn him away from the church we were attending together. I stayed put. But, through this new church is when he really surrendered his whole being to the Lord and really plugged into his relationship with Jesus.

However, dealing with the diabetes was a constant struggle for him. He buckled down and lost a lot of weight and was able to stop the insulin; but then he got a virus which had to be treated with steroids which sent his sugar count to the top so they put him back on insulin and he started putting on the weight he had lost. This weight gain which he had tried so hard to lose threw him into a devil may care attitude about the whole diabetes thing.

The last year of his life he started having transient global amnesia attacks. I had never heard of this condition until the doctor diagnosed it. I believe it was caused by the uncontrolled diabetes. This frustrated my husband even more because he was a very active person and worked a lot with his hands refurbishing old motorcycles. He would forget how to do tasks that he had done for years. Then he started having a lot of pain in his legs; and sometimes they would just give out on him and he would fall to the ground. The doctors of course wanted to put him on Vicodin for the pain, but he refused to take a narcotic. Like myself, he did not believe in taking these kinds of drugs. He suffered a lot with the pain.

He starting praying that God would take him. This frustrated me and made me angry because I did not want to lose him. I thought he could overcome it. I was being selfish. He was at this stage miserable, physically and mentally.

We made an appointment to see what was causing the leg pain, but he never made it; he died four days before. That morning of the day he died, he was in a very agitated state over some financial issues. He was not feeling well, I wanted him to see the doctor; but, he refused. I went off to work because I had a meeting in Baton Rouge. I checked in with him multiple times during the day. One of my sons-in-law checked on him and tried to get him to go to the ER, but once again he refused. He went by a business that one of his friends owned; and I found out later that they wanted to call the ambulance, but he left and would not go. I believe he knew that day that he was going to die, and he wanted no one to stop it. He was tired of living. I found out later after his death that in the month or so before his death, he had gone around making amends with people he thought he had wronged.

On the way home from work that evening, I was stopped in construction traffic when I received a call from my daughter that Tom had passed. My son-in-law had gone back to the house to check on him and found him dead on the bathroom floor. He had had a massive heart attack. We would have been married 31 years in two months. He was 57 years old.

When I got home, my pastor and one of the deacons were there. His body was still in the bathroom, I gave instruction for which funeral home to call to come get the body. I went in and said my goodbyes to him.

In the first days that followed, I was angry with him. I blamed him for wanting to die and leaving me to deal with the finances and everything else by myself. The children were all grown and lived on their own. I asked God why He let this happen. God responded. He told me that I was being selfish, that He honored Tom's wishes to die to spare him from the pain he was living with everyday. He also showed me that the faith I had would grow even stronger and the finances and needs would be taken care of, not to worry.

That conversation with the Lord changed my life. I realized I was being selfish, I was grieving over me not having my husband around anymore. I realized that the Lord had showed mercy on him and I knew that he knew Jesus and was now in Heaven with Him; no more pain, no more diabetes; no more being miserable. When you love someone and you know they know Jesus, you have to let them go when it's time. My faith did grow stronger. Instead of turning from God, I drew closer to Him. Tom died on a Thursday, I was in church on Sunday morning worshiping the Lord. What better place to be than with my Lord and my church family. Did I grieve, yes. That is a natural part of losing a loved one, but it could not rob the joy I had that only the Lord can give. My oldest daughter asked how I was able to deal with it. I said, you take one day at a time.

Tom's body died, but his spirit and soul went immediately to be with the Lord. What a wonderful peace knowing that.

Just as God had told me, the finances and business matters fell into place. God poured his blessings out upon me. God did not wave a magic wand and made everything right; He guided me in the direction of how to take care of things. It is a two-way street, we do our part, God does His.

IX

A year after Tom went to be with the Lord, Hurricane Katrina hit New Orleans. I evacuated to my oldest daughter's house in Illinois. I was displaced for a while. My office in New Orleans was swamped with water up to the third floor, my work was relocated to Baton Rouge which is a two-hour drive from where I was living, taking in the traffic. But, the Lord had not forgotten me. My house had no water damage, very little wind damage. Christian families in the Baton Rouge area were opening up their homes to people like me who had been displaced. The secretary of my church found a family for me to stay with so I would not have to drive everyday back and forth to Baton Rouge. Rent was at a premium, I could not afford to pay rent on my house in New Orleans and on another one in Baton Rouge. The young family welcomed me into their home, having never met me before. They made me feel at home. They had two children, the son who was middle school age at the time gave up his bedroom for me. I would stay with them from Sunday night to Friday, and go home on weekends. I stayed with them for about three months until my work found us temporary office space back in the New Orleans area.

Two months after Katrina, my landlord gave me notice he had sold the house in which I was living. He wanted me out quickly, this was about a week before Thanksgiving; and like I said before, property was at a premium and rental property was hard to find. What at one time would have rented for $500 a month was now renting for $1400. I prayed about it, the Lord provided me with a place., right across from my son's house. The house belonged to his

girlfriend who had moved, and I only had to pay the amount
of her house note which was quite reasonable for that time.

X

While I had been in Illinois at my daughter's, a cousin of my husband's (quite a bit older), contacted me and wanted to donate some money to help out with the Katrina situation. He lived in a town not far from my daughter's, so we made arrangements to meet at his house. I had only seen him twice in the many years Tom and I were married; once at my husband's Grandma's funeral, and then he came to Tom's funeral. He was my mother-in-law's first cousin. We had a good visit and exchanged email addresses and phone numbers. Once I got back to New Orleans, we started communicating by email; and out of the blue one Saturday night I decided to call him just to talk. After that, we talked pretty much everyday. We talked a lot about the Lord. He accepted Jesus as his Lord and Savior and he was hungry to know more about Him. He had been widowed for ten years and was mad at God after his wife died, and stopped praying until one night he said he heard God tell him enough is enough. What many times later became something for us to chuckle about was he asked God to send him a lady who would teach him the Bible, be a companion, and would also be nice if she liked to play golf. In December 2005, we started a relationship. I had not been looking for another man, but God had other ideas. In February 2006, I took an early retirement package and moved back to Illinois. We became a couple.

The funniest part is the golf. I had always thought golf was a stupid game and would make sarcastic remarks about it when I saw it on the TV while surfing channels. One day Ralph and I were sitting on the patio; and out of the blue I said, "I think I would like to learn to play golf". I thought where did that come from. Well, I learned to play golf. God answered Ralph's prayer, most importantly for someone to teach him the Bible, and threw in the golf for good measure. God is like that. He cares about what we care about.

We finally got married in 2010, he laughingly said he didn't realize I would stand my ground so well. His biggest concern was our age different. He was 28 years older than me. I have never looked at that as a stumbling block. I always say that age is a state of mind. He was in great physical shape, lot better than most 40yr. olds. My Dad was 32 years older than my mother. They were married 23 years before he passed. He was 65 when I was born.

Ralph was my champion, my cheerleader. He would embarrass me sometimes with his bragging about my knowing the Bible and my teaching and preaching. He always supported me in the ministries the Lord has blessed me with, traveled with me, and encouraged me. We had a lot of fun together hiking trails, living on the beach in the winter, being a PawPaw and a Grandpa Ralphie to my Grandchildren. We prayed together, studied together, laughed together, cried together.

Ralph went to be with the Lord in December 20019, one week before Christmas. I think it caught me a little off guard because he always seemed bigger than life. He had had a serious hospitalization the year before, which the doctors did not think he would survive (the only one, except for a minor procedure, in the all the time we were together); but I had the faith God would heal him, and he did - at 94 years of age. But, there comes a time for everything. His body was tired, I watched him peacefully just go to sleep and move into the loving arms of his Jesus - a young 95. I miss him terribly, but I rejoice for the years that God blessed us with together and am happy that he is dancing and praising before the Lord.

And, I know that one day I will get to see both Ralph and
Tom again when I go to be with the Lord.

The Lord blessed me with two great marriages, two men as different as night and day. The Lord has a sense of humor. I cannot even imagine losing such a love one and not knowing the Lord. They have no hope. My relationship with Jesus comforts me in this time of grief. Even my mother, after having lost three children, never to my knowledge was angry at the Lord about it. She had faith in God. Even though the trauma she faced as a young child had a big influence on how she looked at life, she came to know Jesus and put her trust in Him. Even though we had our differences, mostly from out different outlooks on life, I remember how she handled death. I can't imagine any greater loss than to lose a child.

God gave his only Son, placed Him on the Cross, so that an unworthy, sinful world might be saved and have a relationship with Him.